Poppy's Christmas Garden

by Siân Lewis

pictures by Gloria

'Dad,' said Poppy, 'Do you know what I want for Christmas?'
'What ?' asked Dad.
'A garden,' said Poppy. 'A garden as big as the world.'

'As big as the world!' gasped Dad falling back in his chair
with his legs in the air in surprise.

You see, Dad and Poppy lived in a flat in the middle of a town. Their flat didn't even have the tiniest patch of earth outside.

Poppy climbed on to Dad's knee.

'Can you get me a garden please, Dad?' she asked.

'A garden as big as the world?' asked Dad looking
worried for a moment. Then he said: 'All right, Poppy, I'll
see what I can do.'

When Poppy woke up on Christmas morning, she knew at once that Dad had bought her the garden.

From the foot of her bed came a tiny noise, the tiny noise of flowers whispering, the noise that seeds make when they slither and slide.

Poppy bounced up and saw a large green parcel on her bed. She pulled the paper off it quick as a flash. Inside the paper was a long white plastic flower pot. Inside the pot was a sack of compost and behind the compost, two packets of chattering seeds.

When Poppy saw what those seeds were, she laughed.
'They're poppies!' she giggled. 'Dad! They're poppies just
like me.'

9

'There's one packet of Red Poppy seeds and one packet of Yellow Poppy seeds,' called a sleepy voice, and into the room came Dad with a smaller candle-shaped parcel in his hand. 'Happy Christmas, prettiest Poppy of all,' he said, tossing the parcel on to the bed.

Poppy caught the parcel just before it rolled on to the floor. She tugged at the paper and out popped a wooden gnome with a smiling face. In one hand he carried a tiny real watering can. In the other a matching trowel, fork and rake.

Poppy and Dad started planting their garden straight after Christmas, when Poppy had finished playing with her Father Christmas toys. They shook the compost into the box. Poppy dug it over with Mr Gnome's fork. She raked it flat.

Then with the tip of the trowel she drew two lines along the middle of the box. In one line she planted Red Poppy seeds. In the other she planted Yellow Poppy seeds. She covered them all with a blanket of compost and watered them with the can.

Poppy put her garden on the kitchen windowsill, where it fitted very neatly — because it wasn't quite as big as the world yet.

'Will it grow?' asked Poppy.

'You wait and see,' said Dad.

Soon tiny green leaves started poking up through the soil in Poppy's garden. They were squashed so close together they could hardly breathe. Dad winked at Poppy.

Together they went down to the garden shop. They bought two more long plastic pots, one brown, one green. They bought two more sacks of compost.

Carefully Poppy lifted some of the squashed plants from her garden and put them in the new pots. She left the brown pot on the living-room windowsill and the green pot on the bathroom shelf.

Poppy's garden was growing. But it still wasn't as big as the world.

Then one morning in early summer, something waved to
Poppy from the windowsill, something soft and floating
with a face as bright as the sun.
'Daddy!' yelled Poppy.

Dad came running in with toothpaste all over his chin.
'Daddy!' yelled Poppy. 'My yellow poppy's opened!'
Dad gave Poppy a hug.

Before long Poppy's windowsills were full of dancing poppies and everyone in the street was stopping to have a look.

'Oh! Aren't those poppies lovely?' they said. And Poppy laughed, because she was a poppy too.

But when autumn came, no-one stopped any more. The red and yellow petals of Poppy's flowers had all fallen off. Only the heads were left, little green heads wobbling in the breeze.
Still Poppy didn't mind. She knew that in those green heads there were fresh new seeds.

One day in late October, when the heads were brown and dry, Dad and Poppy collected the seeds. The tiny black seeds bounced and skipped all over the windowsill, but Poppy managed to catch most of them and put them in a plastic bottle.

'OK?' said Dad.

He winked at Poppy and Poppy winked back.

They both put on their warmest clothes. Dad carried a sharp stick and Poppy carried the plastic bottle.

Together Dad and Poppy walked round the town. Wherever they saw a tiny forgotten bit of earth, Dad made holes with his stick and Poppy emptied seeds inside.

When springtime came, red and yellow poppies burst out all over town. They burst from cracks between old paving stones, from quiet gloomy corners of the park, from little holes in walls.

Poppy's garden had grown as big as the town itself.
And Poppy's garden is still growing.

Soon it'll be as big as the world.
It really will!
You look out in spring and summer.
Can you see red and yellow poppies in the fields near
your house?

If you can, you'll know they're part of . . .
Poppy's Christmas garden!